Ed Cobham

summersdale

Summersdale Publishers Ltd
46 West Street
Chichester
PO19 1RP UK

www.summersdale.com

ISBN 1 84024 259 0
Printed and bound in the UK.

Disclaimer
The majority of these jokes are based on material that is freely available in the public domain. No information as to who wrote the original versions of these jokes was available. If anyone feels they have a valid claim to the copyright ownership of the roots of any joke contained herein, please contact the publishers with supporting evidence in order that credit may be given in any future edition.

Thanks to...

...all my mates who contributed their fave jokes to this nifty little book, making my job a lot easier. These are the people to whom I am particularly indebted and, naturally, owe a beer or two: Ash Gordon, Dr Mojo, Tam Howard, Nutmeg Charley, Bill McMunt, Wazzer, Jed, Pete, Johnno, Frankie, Steve, Ian, Posh Locks, Phat Twat, Hairy Kunt and Turnip. You're a bunch of filthy fuckers and I love you for it.

DIRTY CONTENTS

My husband came home with a tube of KY jelly and said, 'This will make you happy tonight'. He was right. When he went out of the bedroom, I squirted it all over the doorknobs. He couldn't get back in.

**What's the difference
between hard and light?**

**You can sleep
with a light on.**

What's the difference between oral sex and anal sex?

Oral sex makes your day; anal sex makes your hole weak.

DIRTY * DIRTY * DIRTY * DIRTY

Three men are marooned on an island desperately seeking a way to get off. A cannibal approaches them and flops his penis out. 'If the length of your three penises together is as big as mine, then I'll show you how to get off the island. Otherwise you'll be killed and eaten.' The native's nob was an incredible 20 inches. Getting off to a good start, the first man shows off his impressive 10 inches. The second man produces a 9-inch dick. Feeling confident, they urge the third man to get his tackle out. He does so and reveals just one inch of manhood. After some nail-biting calculations the cannibal says, 'Okay fellas, you've managed to come up with the goods: I'll let you use my boat to escape'. As they were sailing to safety, the first bloke mentions how lucky they are that he's so well endowed. Likewise, the second bloke suggests that they are truly blessed at the length of his schlong. The third guy pipes up '...and you're damn lucky I had an erection!'

**Why do farts
smell so bad?**

**So the deaf can
enjoy them too.**

A couple was getting frisky in a field. After giving her oral sex he said, 'Wow, I wish I had a torch'. 'So do I,' she said. 'You've been eating grass for the past ten minutes.'

DIRTY * DIRTY * DIRTY * DIRTY * DIRTY

A guy was sitting in a bar when a stranger walked up to him and asked: 'If you woke up in the woods and scratched your arse and felt *Vaseline*, would you tell anyone?' 'Of course not!' the guy said. The stranger then asked: 'If you felt further into your crack and pulled out a used condom, would you tell anyone?' 'Nope.' 'Great,' said the stranger. 'Fancy going camping then?!'

Little Johnny comes into the house for dinner after playing outside all afternoon. His parents ask him what he did today. He says that he played football and then he proposed to his friend Emily. His parents think this is really sweet and they don't want to make fun of Little Johnny so they ask him, 'How are you both going to pay for the expenses of being married?' 'Well with the £5 I get each week from you and the 50p she gets from her Mum and Dad, we should do okay.' His father says, 'That's fine, but how will you pay the extra expenses if you have a baby?' Little Johnny answers, 'Well, so far – touch wood – we've been lucky...'

A man goes to his wife and says: 'Darling, we are partners. We have been since we got married. We shared the good times, so now there's a problem, and I'm hoping we can share that too.' 'What's the problem?' she asks. 'We got our secretary pregnant and she's suing us for support.'

A young couple is staying at a nudist campsite. 'When I tell you I love you,' asks the young man, 'why do you always lower your eyes?'

'To see if it's true.'

A man returns from a doctor's visit one day and tells his wife that the doctor said he only has 24 hours to live. Wiping away her tears, he asks her to make love to him. Naturally she agrees and they make passionate love. Six hours later he pipes up 'Honey, now I only have 18 hours left to live. Maybe we could make love again?' The loving wife consents and again they find themselves making love. Later, as he is getting into bed he realises he only has 8 hours of life left. He taps his wife's shoulder and says, 'Sweetie-Honey-Darling? Please? Just one more time before I die'. She agrees but rolls over and falls asleep from all that sexual fatigue. The persistent husband, however, hears his internal clock ticking. He tosses and turns

DIRTY * DIRTY * DIRTY * DIRTY * DIRTY

until he has only 4 more hours left to live. Waking her, he urges 'PLEASE! Could we...?' At which point she snaps: 'I have to get up in the morning! You don't!'

A young man was struggling to decide what to wear to a fancy dress party, but eventually had a brain wave. When the host answered the door to find the guest standing there in his Y-fronts he asked him what he was supposed to be? 'Premature ejaculation – I just came in my pants!'

Why did the blonde cross the road?

Who cares? What's she doing out of the bedroom?

DIRTY * DIRTY * DIRTY * DIRTY

A young boy went to visit his grandparents. He noticed his grandfather sitting in a rocking chair with nothing on from the waist down. 'Gramps, what are you doing?' he exclaimed. The old man looked off in the distance and did not answer him. 'Gramps, what are you doing sitting out here with nothing on below the waist?' he asked again. The old man slowly looked at him and said, 'Well, last week I sat out here with no shirt on, and I got a stiff neck. This is Granny's idea'.

What does an 80-year-old
woman have between
her knees that a young
woman doesn't?

Her tits.

DIRTY * DIRTY * DIRTY * DIRTY

Little Red Riding Hood was walking through the woods one day, when she spied the big bad wolf crouched down behind a bush. Thinking that it would be funny to sneak up on him for once, she crept over and tapped him on his shoulder.

'Mister Wolf,' she smirked. 'What big eyes you have.'

'Leave me alone', said the wolf running off.

'What big ears you have', she continued whilst following deeper into the woods.

'Please leave me alone', he howled desperately trying to get her off his case.

Persistent Little Red Riding Hood ran after the wolf to discover him in a patch of bracken.

'Mister Wolf, what big teeth you have.'

'Fuckin' hell, just leave me alone,' he angrily barked. 'Can't you see I'm trying to have a poo?'

DIRTY * DIRTY * DIRTY * DIRTY

What's the difference between love, true love and showing off?

Spitting, swallowing and gargling.

What's the difference between erotic and kinky?

Erotic is when you use a feather; kinky is when you use the whole chicken.

DIRTY * DIRTY * DIRTY * DIRTY

What have a *Cartier* watch and David Beckham got in common?

Both come in a posh box.

What do peroxide blondes and aeroplanes have in common?

Both have big black boxes.

DIRTY * DIRTY * DIRTY * DIRTY

A man was in hospital for a series of tests, the last of which left his digestive system slightly worse for wear. Upon making several false alarm trips to the loo, he figured that he might as well stay put. Suddenly, however, he shat in his bed and was embarrassed beyond his ability to remain rational. In a complete loss of composure he jumped out of bed, gathered up the sheets and threw them out the hospital window. A drunk was walking by the hospital when the sheets landed on him. The drunk started yelling, cursing and swinging his arms violently in an attempt to free himself of the bed linen. He ended up with the soiled sheets in a tangled pile at his feet. As he stood there staring down at the sheets, a hospital security guard (who had witnessed the entire faecal incident) walked up to him and asked, 'What the hell is going on?' The drunk, still staring down at the sheets, replied, 'I think I just beat the shit out of a ghost'.

A tourist was visiting a small fishing village and noticed there was a local fisherman with a head no larger than a light bulb. So he asked him, 'Why is your head so small?' 'Well, many years ago,' replied the mutant-headed local, 'I caught a mermaid in my net. I was going to sell her to the marine biologists but she begged and pleaded, saying that she would grant me three wishes if I set her free.' 'What did you wish for?' asked the intrigued tourist. 'Firstly, a beautiful new fishing boat and was stunned when a new trawler appeared. Then I asked for immense wealth. And immediately the deck of my boat was covered with gold coins and jewels. Thirdly, I asked for a good, long shag with the mermaid.'

Naturally, the tourist was desperate to know if the local's final wish was granted and asked what the mermaid's response was. 'When she pointed out that she was only half a woman, I asked for a little head instead.'

A young man walks into the Patent Office with a couple of his latest inventions under his arms: 'I'd like to register my new invention – a folding bottle.' 'Very interesting,' says the clerk. 'What do you call it?' 'A *fottle*,' replies the young inventor. 'That's a pretty silly name, can't you think of something else?' asks the clerk. 'I'll think about it. In the meantime, I've got something else here to show you: my invention for a folding carton.' 'And what do you call that?' asks the clerk. 'Oh, this is what I call a *farton*,' replies our young inventor. 'That is much too rude, you can't possibly use that name,' says the clerk. 'Damn, I guess you're going to hate the name of my folding bucket then.'

A young man with a particularly small penis takes his girlfriend to bed for the first time. Embarrassed at his lack of nob, he insists on turning out the light. In the darkness, he puts his erection into her hand and is understandably hurt when she says, 'No thanks, I don't smoke'.

DIRTY * DIRTY * DIRTY * DIRTY

An elderly man shuffles into a chemist and asks for *Viagra*. 'No problem,' says the pharmacist. 'How much do you want?' 'Just four,' replies the old geezer. 'But could you cut them into tiny pieces? I'm not interested in sex. I just want to be able to piss without hitting my slippers.'

A blonde was in a sex shop and stopped at the dildo counter. 'I'd like that nice fat tartan one with the white top,' she politely asked the shop attendant, who replied: 'It's not for sale, love. That's my thermos flask.'

DIRTY * DIRTY * DIRTY * DIRTY

A man is having problems with his dick, which certainly had seen better times. He consults a doctor who, after a couple of tests, says, 'Sorry, but you've overdone it the last 30 years. Your dick is burned out. You only have 30 erections left in your penis'. The man walks home, deeply depressed. His wife is waiting for him at the front door and he tells her what the doc told him. She says, 'Oh no! Only 30 times! We shouldn't waste that! We should make a list!' He replies, 'I already made a list on the way home, and I'm afraid your name isn't on it'.

A couple of teenage boys walk into their local chemist and ask for a packet of tampons. 'Are they for your mum?' asks the man behind the counter. 'No. They're for us,' reply the boys. 'Why?' asks the baffled man behind the counter. ' It says on TV that you can swim, surf, dive, play tennis, rollerblade *and* ride horses if you use tampons.'

Two old ladies were smoking a cigarette while waiting for a bus. It started to rain, so one of them reached into her purse, took out a condom, cut off the tip, slipped it over her cigarette and continued to smoke. Her friend saw this and said, 'Hey, that's a good idea! What is it that you put over your cigarette?' The other old lady said, 'It's a condom'. 'A condom? Where do you get those?' The lady with the dry cigarette told her friend, 'You can purchase condoms at the pharmacy'. When the two old ladies arrived back in their hometown, the old lady with all the questions went into the pharmacy and asked the man behind the counter, 'Do you sell condoms?' The pharmacist said, 'Yes' but looked a little surprised that this old woman was still sexually active. So he asked her, 'What size do you want?' The old lady thought for a minute and said, 'One that will fit a Camel'.

What's the difference between a woman with her period and a terrorist?

You can negotiate with a terrorist.

Why do men have
a hole in the end
of their nob?

To get air to
their brain.

DIRTY * DIRTY * DIRTY * DIRTY

A bear and a bunny are sitting in a forest taking a shit. The bear leans over to the bunny and asks, 'Do you ever get shit sticking to your fur?' The fluffy bunny says, 'No, Mr Bear. Never'. So the bear grabs the bunny and wipes his arse.

Adrunk walks into the bar carrying a small case. He puts the case on the bar and says to the barman, 'I bet you a double scotch I can show you the most amazing thing you've ever seen'. 'I've seen some pretty amazing things in my time,' says the barman 'but I accept the bet'. The drunk opens his case and there inside is a pianist - just 12 inches tall - sitting down playing a piano. 'I've never seen anything like it,' said the barman. 'Where did you get that?' 'Well,' says the proud owner of this musical phenomenon, 'I dug up this old lamp and when I rubbed it a genie appeared and said I could have one wish'. 'What did you ask for?' asks the fascinated barman. 'A twelve inch penis…'

A man meets a gorgeous woman in a bar. There is an obvious attraction between them and they end up leaving together. They get back to her place and, as she shows him around her apartment, he notices that her bedroom is completely packed with teddy bears. Hundreds of small bears fill a shelf the length of the wall; medium-sized ones adorn a shelf a little higher, and huge bears sit side by side on the top shelf. The man is surprised that this sexy woman should own so many cuddly toys, but he decides not to let it bother him. Instead, he turns to her and kisses her passionately on the lips. After just seconds they are ripping each other's clothes off and having wet and wild sex. After their intense sex session they are lying there together in the afterglow and the man asks, 'Well, love, how was it?' She says, 'You can have any prize from the bottom shelf'.

**What do you get
when you cross a naughty
dog with a rooster?**

**A cock that
won't come.**

DIRTY * DIRTY * DIRTY * DIRTY * DIRTY

Little Johnny asks his mum, 'Where do babies come from?'
'The stork brings them, Johnny.'
Confused Little Johnny then asks, 'Who fucks the stork then, Mummy?'

A blind man is travelling in his private jet when he detects something wrong. He makes his way to the cockpit to discover his pilot dead. He radios the control tower who ask, 'What's the problem?' The blind guy yells, 'Help me! I'm blind... the pilot is dead and we're flying upside down!' The people in the control tower ask, 'How do you know you're upside down?' 'Because the shit is running down my back!'

A middle aged man, about 5 foot 8 inches tall, walks into a pharmacy and furtively asks if they sell *Viagra*. The pharmacist answers firmly, 'Yes, sir. We certainly do.' The man then asks, 'Do you think I could get it over the counter?' The pharmacist thinks for a moment and then says, 'If you took 5 or 6 pills at once you might.'

An elderly man goes into a brothel and tells the madam he would like a young girl for the night. Surprised, she looks at the ancient man and asks how old he is. 'I'm 90 years old,' he says. '90!' replies the woman. 'Don't you realise you've had it?' 'Oh, sorry,' says the old man, 'how much do I owe you?'

DIRTIER * DIRTIER * DIRTIER * DIRTIER * DIRTIER

Three men are chatting about their girlfriends. The Italian man says, 'When I've a finisheda makina da love with my girlfriend I go down and gently tickle the back of her knees. She floatsa 6 inches above da bed in ecstasy'. His French friend replies, 'Zat is nothing, when Ah 'ave finished making ze love with ze girlfriend Ah kiss all ze way down her body and zen Ah lick zer soles of her feet wiz mah tongue and she floats 12 inches above ze bed in pure ecstasy'. Their Aussie mate adds, 'Mate, that's nothing. When I've finished shaggin' my chick, I get out of bed, walk over to the window and wipe me dick on the curtains. She hits the fuckin' roof!'

Two married buddies are out drinking one night when one turns to the other and says, 'You know, I don't know what else to do. Whenever I go home after we've been out drinking I turn the headlights off before I get to the driveway. I shut off the engine and quietly coast into the garage. I take my shoes off before I go into the house, I sneak up the stairs, I get undressed in the bathroom, I ease into bed and my wife STILL wakes up and yells at me for staying out so late!' His buddy looks at him and says, 'Well, you're obviously taking the wrong approach. I screech into the driveway, slam the door, storm up the steps, throw my shoes into the wardrobe, jump into bed, rub my hands on my wife's arse and say, "How about a blow job?"...And she's always sound asleep'.

Little Johnny runs into the farmhouse where his mum and grandma are shelling peas. He yells, 'Mum! The bull's fucking the cow!' Grandma gasps and clutches her chest in horror. Mum drags Little Johnny outside by the scruff of his neck and says, 'Now listen here Johnny, you can't go around saying rude words like that! You have to think up another word instead. How about the bull is SURPRISING the cow?' So Little Johnny is a bit confused, but he shrugs and runs off outside to play again. Five minutes later he runs back inside and shouts: 'Mum! The bull is SURPRISING all of the cows now!' Mum sighs and says to Johnny, 'No, Johnny. He can't be SURPRISING all the cows at once!' 'Yes he is!' yells Little Johnny 'He's SURPRISING all of the cows . . . He's fucking the horse!'

DIRTIER * DIRTIER * DIRTIER * DIRTIER * DIRTIER * DIRTIER

An elderly couple met and fell in love. As they started getting off with each other for the first time she confessed: 'I have acute angina', hoping that it wouldn't dampen his lust. 'That'll make up for your droopy tits then,' he said.

What's the difference between a clitoris and the mini bar in a hotel?

Most men can find the mini bar in less than 3 minutes.

Two men are comparing notes on their wives, one of whom is particularly sporty. 'Haven't you ever seen her wrestle?' asks one of the men. 'No, but I've seen her box a few times.'

What happened to the girl who went fishing with a group of men?

She returned home with a red snapper.

DIRTIER * DIRTIER * DIRTIER * DIRTIER

Aman goes to a tattoo artist and says: 'I'd like you to tattoo a one-hundred pound note onto my dick.' The tattoo artist is surprised: 'Well, that could hurt a lot. Why would you want a one-hundred pound note on your dick?' The man answers, 'Three reasons: I like to watch my money grow; I like to play with my money; **and** next time my wife wants to blow a hundred quid she won't have to leave the house!'

What do parsley
and pubic hair
have in common?

You just push it
aside and keep
on eating!

A priest was taking a shower in the church and ran out of soap. Thinking the church was empty, he walked naked down the hall to the supply closet. On the way back, the naked priest saw three nuns walking towards him. He immediately froze and pretended to be a statue. The first nun took one look and said, 'What a realistic looking statue!' The second nun reached and felt the priest's dick and he dropped a bar of soap in shock. 'Wow a dispenser!' she exclaimed. The third nun reached over, pulled on his dick and said, 'Ooh! Hand Cream too!'

What's the similarity between a mobile phone and a clitoris?

Both turn on with the touch of a finger and every cunt's got one.

A man walked into the bar and there was a gorilla sitting on a barstool. The man asked the bartender what the gorilla was doing in the bar so the bartender showed him. He took out a bat and hit the gorilla over the head with it. The animal instantly dropped down and gave the bartender a blow job. The bartender then asked the man if he would like to try it. 'Sure, but please don't hit me quite so hard.'

**What's the best thing
about a blow job?**

5 minutes' silence.

DIRTIER * DIRTIER * DIRTIER * DIRTIER * DIRTIER

Two drunks had just been thrown out of the bar and are walking down the street when they come across a dog, sitting on the curb and licking his balls. They stood there watching and after a while one of them said, 'I sure wish I could do that!' The other one looks at him and said, 'Well, I think I'd at least pet him first'.

Why does Father Christmas make an ideal lover?

Because he fills your stocking.

DIRTIER * DIRTIER * DIRTIER * DIRTIER

An elderly, married couple walks into a hospital. The doctor says to the old man, 'I'll need a urine sample, a faeces sample, and a blood sample.' The old man says, 'What?' So the doctor says it again. Once again the deaf old codger says, 'What?' So the doctor yells it: 'I NEED A URINE SAMPLE, A FAECES SAMPLE, AND A BLOOD SAMPLE!' With that the old man's wife turns to her doddery husband and says, 'He needs a pair of your underwear, darling!'

What's the difference
between an egg
and a wank?

You can beat an egg,
but you sure can't
beat a wank.

DIRTIER * DIRTIER * DIRTIER * DIRTIER * DIRTIER

DIRTIER * DIRTIER * DIRTIER * DIRTIER * DIRTIER * DIRTIER

A girl is standing at The Gates of Heaven when she hears horrible screams of pain and torture coming from inside. She says to St. Peter, 'What's going on?' He says, 'That's the sound of new angels getting big holes drilled into their backs for their wings, and small holes drilled into their heads for their halos.' She says, 'Heaven sounds terrible. I think maybe I'd rather go to Hell'. St. Peter says, 'In Hell, you'll be constantly raped and sodomized'. She says, 'That's okay, I've already got holes for that'.

A group of gay men were sitting together in the *Jacuzzi* when a bit of spunk rose to the water's surface. One of them automatically asked, 'Who farted?'

After much consideration, a childless couple decides to try artificial insemination. The woman goes to the clinic for her first appointment and is told to take her knickers off and place her feet in the stirrups. When she is ready the doctor comes in and proceeds to take his pants off too, saying: 'Well, you wanted to get pregnant. We're out of bottled stuff so you'll have to settle for draught!'

DIRTIER * DIRTIER * DIRTIER * DIRTIER * DIRTIER

A young girl visits the doctor, worried about the green marks she's developed between her legs. The doctor asks her to remove her clothing and pop onto the couch for an examination. Upon inspecting her troubled vagina, he says, 'Hmm, I'm familiar with this problem. Have you had sex with a gypsy recently?' Embarrassed (as well she should be), the young girl confesses. The doctor says, 'Thought so. When you see him next, tell him that his earrings aren't made of gold'.

A woman complains to her friend that her husband is losing interest in sex, and that he prefers nights out with the lads to the joys of copulation. Her friend tells her that to win his love she must make more effort. She advises her to cook a slap up meal and then send him drinking with his pals down the pub. When he returns she must be dressed in her naughtiest lingerie to look her sexiest. The following evening the troubled wife does exactly as instructed by her sage friend and is dressed to kill by the time her husband returns home. When he sees her lying on the bed in all her gear, he tells her to stand up and take it all off. He then orders her to do a handstand against the bathroom mirror and open her legs. He has never been so erotic and this really turns her on. She does as he says and is excited as he puts his face between her legs. However, he then quips, 'Oh well, I guess the lads are right. I wouldn't suit a beard after all'.

DIRTIER * DIRTIER * DIRTIER * DIRTIER

Worried about his failing eyesight, a man goes to an optician who orders him to stop masturbating. 'Why? Am I going blind?' he asks worriedly. 'No your eyesight is fine, but it upsets the other patients in the waiting room.'

A woman is frustrated with her love life because her husband has a massive crush on Brigitte Bardot and ignores her completely. To win back his attentions, she goes to a tattooist to have the letters 'BB' tattooed on her breasts. The tattooist warns her that age and gravity willl probably make this unattractive later in life, and suggests she have the tattoo on her arse instead. She agrees, and bends over to receive a 'B' on each buttock. When her husband gets home from work that night she greets him by turning around, bending over, and lifting her dress to expose the artwork. 'What do you think?' the wife asks, seeking his approval. 'Eh, who the fuck is Bob?' the husband replies.

DIRTIER * DIRTIER * DIRTIER * DIRTIER

One day Superman was flying along, feeling kind of horny. He had a busy day ahead of him, but just had to satisfy his urge. So he decided he would fly over to Wonder Woman's house to see what she was doing. As he got closer he used his x-ray vision and, to his surprise, Wonder Women was lying on her bed totally nude. Superman thought, 'This is great! I'll just zip right in there, do my business, and before she knows it, I'll be gone.' So, Superman blasts in, right on top of Wonder Woman, does the deed at light speed, and is gone in a flash. Wonder Woman, not quite knowing what hit her said, 'Jesus H Christ! What was that?' and the Invisible Man replied: 'I don't know, but my arse sure is sore!'

A mother is in the kitchen making supper for her family when her young daughter walks in. 'Mummy, where do babies come from?' After thinking about it for a moment the mother explains, 'Well dear, a girl and a boy fall in love and get married. Then, one night they go into their room, hug and kiss, and have sex'. The child looks puzzled so the mother continues, 'That means that Daddy puts his penis in Mummy's vagina. That's how you get a baby'. The child replies, 'But, the other night when I came into your bedroom, you had Daddy's penis in your mouth. What do you get when you do that, Mummy?' 'Jewellery.'

There's a woman in a hospital in a coma. Her nurse notices after a few days that every time she sponge-bathes the woman around the crotch, the monitor increases significantly. The nurse gets the bright idea that oral sex might just provide the stimulus to bring the woman out of her coma. She calls the woman's husband, tells him her idea and he instantly agrees. When he arrives at the hospital, the nurse ushers him into the room, closes the curtain around the bed and closes the door. Five minutes later, the man comes running out of the room screaming that all of his wife's vital signs have plummeted to zero and she needs a doctor immediately. The nurse, distraught that she was jeopardising the life of the woman she had sought to save, asked the man what had happened. 'I'm not sure, but I think she choked'.

A young woman went to her doctor for a follow-up visit after the doctor had given her a prescription for the male hormone *testosterone*. The woman was a little worried about some of the side effects she was experiencing. 'Doctor, the hormones you've been giving me have really helped, but I'm afraid you're giving me too much. I've started growing hair in places where I've never grown hair before.' The doctor reassured her, 'A little hair growth is a perfectly normal side effect of *testosterone*. Just where has this hair appeared?' The woman replied, 'On my balls'.

Two horny lovers were out in the field merrily fucking away. It had rained that morning and there was lots of mud on the ground, so they found themselves sliding around a bit. 'Honey, is my cock inside you or in the mud?' the man asked. His girlfriend felt around and exclaimed, 'It's in the mud!' 'Well, put it back inside you,' he said. A couple of minutes later he asked, 'Honey, is it inside you or in the mud?' 'It's definitely inside me,' she moaned with ecstasy. 'Well, would you mind putting it back in the mud?'

An old man goes to the doctor asking for a prescription for the strongest dose of *Viagra*, explaining that he has two extremely insatiable young girls spending the weekend with him. He happily toddles off with his prescription. Later that week though, he returns to the doctor asking for painkillers. The doctor asks 'Why, is your dick in pain after all that sex?' 'No', says the geriatric lover-man, 'it's for my wrists - the girls never showed up!'

This lady goes to the gynaecologist but won't tell the receptionist what's wrong with her, just that she must see a doctor. After hours of waiting the doctor sees her in. The doctor asks her what her problem is. 'Well', she says, 'my husband is a very compulsive gambler and every penny that he can get his hands on he gambles. I had £1000, which I stuffed in my vagina but now I can't get it out'. The doctor says, 'Don't be nervous. I see this happen all the time. Please pull down your underwear and put your feet in the stirrups. Just a quick question: What am I looking for? Notes or loose change?'

DIRTIER * DIRTIER * DIRTIER * DIRTIER

A man heard that masturbating before sex often helped blokes last longer during the act. The man decided to give it a try. He spent the rest of the day thinking about where to do it. He couldn't do it in his office, but that was too open. He considered an alley, but figured that was too unsafe. On his way home, he pulled his truck over on the side of the road. He got out and crawled underneath as if he was examining the truck. Satisfied with the privacy, he undid his pants and started to wank. He closed his eyes and thought of his lover. As he grew closer to orgasm, he felt a quick tug at the bottom of his trousers. Not wanting to jeopardise the orgasm, he kept his eyes shut. Then he heard voices: 'This is the police. What's going on down there?' The man replied, 'I'm checking out the rear axle, it's broken'. 'Well, you might as well check your brakes too while you're down there because your truck rolled down the hill 5 minutes ago.'

DIRTIER * DIRTIER * DIRTIER * DIRTIER

Two young lovers are in bed getting frisky when the girl places the guy's hand onto her pussy. 'Put your finger in me...' she requests. So he does without hesitation and she starts moaning with pleasure. 'Put two fingers in', she says. So in goes another one. She's really starting to get worked up and says, 'Put your whole hand in!' He shoves his whole hand up her hole and she begs him to put both your hands inside of me!' He consents without a fuss. 'Now clap your hands', commands the girl. 'I can't', says the guy. The girl looks at him and says 'See, I told you I had a tight pussy!'

A dog, a cat, and a penis are sitting around a campfire one night. The dog says, 'My life sucks, my master makes me do my business on a fire hydrant!' The cat says, 'Well beat this: my master makes me do my business in a box of cat litter'. The outraged penis says, 'At least your master doesn't put a bag over your head and make you do push ups until you throw up!'

What's the difference between a slag and a bowling ball?

You can only get 3 fingers in a bowling ball.

A desperate bloke takes a gorgeous girl out for an expensive meal in the hope that she'll repay him with endless sexual favours. They tuck into their food and she eats with gusto not usually befitting a young lady. He comments on her extraordinarily healthy appetite to which she responds, 'I always eat like a horse when I'm on the blob'.

A young woman goes to the doctor complaining of bad breath. After trying every remedy under the sun, the doctor finally asks her how she has sex. 'Doggy style' she says. He suggests that she try it on her back, to which she huffs, 'Have you ever smelled a German Sheep Dog's breath?'

What do you get if you stand a blonde on her head?

A brunette with bad breath.

Three blokes are comparing their drunkenness from the night before. The first one says, 'I was so drunk I don't even know how I got home…I just woke up in my bed in a pool of sweat.' 'Oh yeah,' brags the second guy, 'I was so wasted I took home a strange woman and was having sex with her when my wife walked in.' 'That's nothing,' said the third. 'I was so pissed that I was blowing chunks all night.' The other two cry in unison, 'Big deal!' 'I don't think you understand,' says bloke number one. 'Chunks is the name of my dog.'

**What do you
call a prostitute
with a runny nose?**

Full.

There was a father who was very proud of his three daughters. Every night he took a stroll around the house to make sure everything was all right. One night, he could hear laughter coming from his youngest daughter's room. When he reached the window of his second daughter, he could hear her crying. There were no sounds at all coming from his oldest daughter's room. The next day, when they were all gathered around the breakfast table, he said to his youngest daughter 'I heard you laughing last night, as I walked past your window. Why was that?' She answered, 'That's because you taught me to laugh when someone was making me happy'. He then asked his second daughter why she was crying. She answered, 'Because you taught me to cry when someone was making me sad'. He then said his oldest daughter 'I didn't hear anything from you', to which she replied: 'That's because you taught me not to talk with my mouth full...'

DIRTIEST * DIRTIEST * DIRTIEST * DIRTIEST

A married couple is snuggling down in bed, the husband gently taps his wife on the shoulder and starts rubbing her arm. His wife turns over and says, 'I'm sorry honey, I've got a gynaecologist appointment tomorrow and I want to stay fresh'. Her husband, rejected, turned over and tries to sleep. A few minutes later, he rolls back over and taps his wife again. 'Do you have a dental appointment tomorrow too?'

After years of flirting a man and a woman in an old people's home agree to make love. Impatient for his first bit of action in decades, the man is anxious to go down on her. However, after just a few seconds of muff-diving the geriatric bird, he reappears saying 'Sorry love, but the smell is just too bad'. 'Oh dear,' she says, 'it must be the arthritis'. 'Arthritis of the front bottom?' he asks with disbelief. 'Are you sure? And surely arthritis doesn't smell?' Setting him straight, she says: 'No darling, the arthritis is in my shoulder. I can't wipe my arse'.

Three rottweilers are talking in the waiting room at the vet's surgery. The first dog says, 'I was out walking with my master when a thug attacked him. I chased the bloke, caught him by the throat and savaged him to death. So I'm here to be put down'.

The second dog says, 'I was in the house when a burglar broke in and tried to nick the TV and stereo, so I pinned him down and bit his arm off. I'm here to be put down too'.

The third dog tells his tale: 'I was patrolling the house one evening and I wandered into the bathroom to see my master's wife naked, bending over the bath. I leapt up and gave her a jolly good seeing to doggy-style'. The other dogs asked pitifully, 'And you're being put down too, right?' 'No, I'm here to get my claws clipped.'

DIRTIEST * DIRTIEST * DIRTIEST * DIRTIEST

A bloke walks into the doctor's surgery looking very sheepish. The doctor asks him what the problem is and he explains that it's a rather delicate matter to do with his back passage, which he finds hard to talk about. The doctor says, 'Look mate, I've been in this profession for 26 years and there isn't much I haven't seen. I know you must be embarrassed but I'm a doctor and it would save us both a lot of time if you told me'. The guy drops his trousers and bends down revealing a bloody and ragged arsehole that looks like it's been under serious attack. The doctor is shocked at what he sees: 'Christ! What happened to you?' The embarrassed patient explains that he was raped by an elephant whilst on safari. 'Hmm, I know I'm not a vet but my limited knowledge in that field tells me that elephant penises are long and thin,' says the doctor. 'You're not wrong there Doc, but he fingered me first.'

DIRTIEST * DIRTIEST * DIRTIEST * DIRTIEST

The wife coyly tried to explain her purchase of a new pair of expensive designer panties. 'After all, dear,' she said to her husband, 'you wouldn't expect to find fine perfume in a cheap bottle, would you?' 'No,' her husband replied. 'Nor would I expect to find gift wrapping on a dead beaver.'

A man went to a brothel to get some practice performing oral sex on his wife. The prozzie was happy to give him a few pointers and then told him to go for it. So the man went down on her and he was, judging by her reaction, pretty good at it. But something strange happened. A couple of minutes into the deed, he felt something in his mouth. He spat it into his hand and found a piece of carrot. 'Yuk!' he thought, but said nothing and continued. A couple of minutes later, he came up with a broad bean. 'Fucking hell. This is revolting,' he thought. Nevertheless, he said nothing and gave her filthy box one more shot. A couple of minutes later he came up with a piece of chicken. He couldn't stand it any longer.

'I can't do this anymore! I'm gonna throw up!' 'That's weird,' remarked the hooker, 'that's just what the last fella did.'

A well known, much-married celebrity said to her doctor, 'I have a new boyfriend and he's 18, so I want you to tighten my vagina. This has to be our secret - no tabloids, definitely no leaks.'

Her doctor was standing there when she woke up after the operation. She looked at the foot of the bed and saw three bouquets of flowers.

She said angrily to the doctor, 'How could you do this to me? I told you this was to be a secret'.

The doctor said, 'Relax. The first bouquet is from me. The second is from the anaesthetist - he worked with me on your operation. He's gay and very trustworthy. He won't tell a soul. And the third bouquet is from a guy in the burns unit who wanted to thank you for his new pair of ears'.

Aformer prostitute with a vagina that has been somewhat stretched from over-use, is given a proposal of marriage by a man she meets in a bar one night. She thinks it over and she decides to accept his hand in marriage. Her hole is rather capacious thanks to her former occupation, but she decides to approach the sensitive issue after they are married. On their wedding night, she explains the problem by saying that when she was a small child, she got her privates caught on some barbed wire while climbing over a fence – hence her massive cavity. They make wild and passionate love for most of the night. In the early hours of the morning her husband (after regaining his breath) turns to her and says, 'I can understand your snatch being stretched by barbed wire, but just HOW far across the field were you before you noticed?'

Little Johnny's mother is taking a bath, having recently been discharged from hospital where she had all of her pubic hair removed. Johnny comes into the bathroom as she is drying off and asks what happened to the hair. 'I've lost my sponge,' she says. A few days later Little Johnny tells his mother that he thinks he's found her sponge. 'Where is it, darling?' asks his proud mummy. 'The lady next door is washing Daddy's face with it.'

Following a hard day in court, a judge decides to go the pub. Several whiskies later, he staggers out of the boozer and starts to walk home. On his way he feels sick and throws up all over his posh suit. Arriving home, he uses his fine legal mind to explain the mess to his wife: 'A filthy tramp vomited all over me'. So, his lovely wife makes him a cup of tea out of sympathy. The next day the judge comes home and decides to make yesterday's story a wee bit more convincing by saying, 'You'll never guess what but that tramp was in court today. I gave him 6 months'. His understanding wife declared, 'Darling you should have given him a year – he shat in your pants as well'.

DIRTIEST * DIRTIEST * DIRTIEST * DIRTIEST

A young woman decided that she wanted to please her boyfriend by wearing some saucy, crotchless knickers. That evening, she lay on the bed waiting for her man to come home. She was totally naked except for her new panties and had her legs wide a part. When he arrived home he raced up to the bedroom where he thought he'd find her. 'Do you fancy some of this?' she said huskily. 'Fuck no, look what it's done to your knickers!'

Walking down an alleyway one night a policeman spots a tramp with his fingers shoved up the arse of another tramp. 'What on earth do you two think you are doing?' The tramp says, 'My good friend here has drunk too much today and I am simply trying to help sick it up'.

The concerned bobby said, 'Sticking your digits up his arse won't do much good'. 'Obviously Officer, but sticking them in his gob afterwards should work a treat.'

DIRTIEST * DIRTIEST * DIRTIEST * DIRTIEST

What do a gynaecologist and a pizza delivery boy have in common?

They can both smell it, but can't eat it.

A man and his wife go to their honeymoon hotel for their 25th anniversary. As the couple reflected on that magical evening 25 years ago, the wife asked the husband, 'When you first saw my naked body in front of you, what was going through your mind?' The husband replied, 'All I wanted to do was to fuck your brains out and suck your tits dry'. Then as the wife was undressing she asked, 'What are you thinking now?' He replied, 'It looks as if I did a pretty good job'.

DIRTIEST * DIRTIEST * DIRTIEST * DIRTIEST

Other titles from Summersdale

THE LITTLE BOOK OF
STUDENT BOLLOCKS

JOSEPH GELFER

HISTORY

summersdale *humour*

THE LITTLE BOOK OF

DRINKING GAMES

FOR ADULTS ONLY!

summersdale *humour*

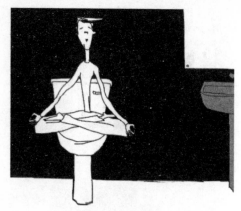

THE LITTLE BOOK OF

DUM - PING

ACHIEVING HARMONY THROUGH TOILET YOGA

MICHAEL POWELL

summersdale *humour*

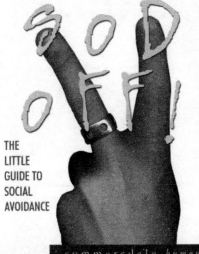

IRENE GRAHAM

SOD OFF!

**THE
LITTLE
GUIDE TO
SOCIAL
AVOIDANCE**

summersdale *humour*

HOW TO CHAT-UP
BABES
Your place or mine?
You go to yours...
I'll go to mine.
STEWART FERRIS
summersdale humour

HOW TO CHAT-UP
BLOKES
Want to come with me for a pizza and a kiss?
No thanks. Don't like pizza.
KITTY MALONE & BUNNY SYLVESTER
summersdale humour

EMMA
BURGESS

THE LITTLE BOOK OF

ESSENTIAL
FOREIGN
INSULTS

summersdale *humour*

EMMA
BURGESS

THE LITTLE BOOK OF

ESSENTIAL
FOREIGN
SWEAR
WORDS

summersdale *humour*

sexy

French

How to:
* seduce a Frenchie
* get rid of them in the morning
* tell the doctor where it itches

Emma Burgess

summersdale *humour*